Using Word

for beginners

Linda Steven

WHSMITH LTD, SWINDON, WILTS. SN3 3LD
In association with:

PEARSON EDUCATION LIMITED
Head Office:
Edinburgh Gate, Harlow, Essex CM20 2JE
Tel: +44 (0)1279 623623 Fax: +44 (0)1279 431059

London Office:
128 Long Acre, London WC2E 9AN
Tel: +44 (0)207 447 2000 Fax: +44 (0)207 240 5771
Website: www.it-minds.com

First published in Great Britain 2001
© Pearson Education Limited 2001

British Library Cataloguing in Publication Data
A CIP catalogue record for this book can be obtained from the British Library.

ISBN 0-130-65283-0

10 9 8 7 6 5 4 3 2 1

Typeset by Pantek Arts Ltd, Maidstone, Kent.
Printed and bound in Great Britain by Ashford Colour Press, Gosport, Hampshire.

The publishers' policy is to use paper manufactured from sustainable forests.

contents

introduction

Word is the most widely used Windows word processor, and Word 2000 contains many improvements that make it even more user-friendly. This book is designed to give you a general idea of how to use Word 2000 to improve the quality, speed and enjoyment of your work.

There are icons throughout the book and these indicate notes that will give you more detail on certain points or explain new ideas. Each icon tells you what type of information the note provides (see below).

+info *These notes provide additional information about a subject.*

These notes indicate shortcuts and techniques reserved for experts.

These notes warn you of potential risks, and show you how to avoid pitfalls.

If you've not used Word 2000 before then it's best to read the chapters in order, starting with the basics, e.g. how to install the Word 2000 program and how to call up an 'Office Assistant' icon (whose role it is to answer any queries you have). If you're familiar with Word then simply jump straight to the chapter you're interested in.

I

Discovering the software

Installing Word 2000

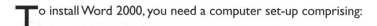

To install Word 2000, you need a computer set-up comprising:

● a Pentium or a DX 400;

● Windows 95 or 98;

● at least 16 MB of RAM (random access memory, or main memory)

● a hard disk;

● a CD-ROM drive;

● a Windows-compatible screen;

● a Microsoft-compatible mouse.

To install Word 2000, perform the following steps:

1 Switch on your computer and start Windows.

2 Insert the Word 2000 disk into your CD-ROM drive.

3 Select the **Installation** button.

4 Follow the instructions that appear in the program installation dialogue boxes.

*If you use Word frequently, add a shortcut to your desktop to bypass the Start menu: click with the right-hand mouse button (right-click) on the **Microsoft Word** entry in the **Programs** submenu and drag it on to the desktop. In the context menu that opens on the desktop, select **Create Shortcut(s) Here**.*

Starting Word 2000

Click on the **Start** icon on the taskbar at the bottom of the screen, and select **Programs**. Then click on **Microsoft Word** (Fig. 1.1).

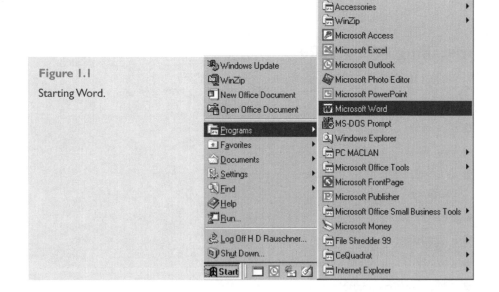

Figure 1.1

Starting Word.

Configuring Word 2000

Configuring your word processor means adapting it to your own requirements.

Fonts

A font is a set of characters with the same typeface. For this example, we will select the Book Antiqua font:

1 In Word, click on **Format**.

2 Select the **Font** option.

3 Click on the **Font** tab, and scroll down the list of fonts.

4 Click on **Book Antiqua**, then **OK** (Fig. 1.2).

Now select the size of your font. We will use 10. You can proceed in one of two ways.

On the Formatting toolbar, click the arrow to the right of the **Font Size** box, then scroll down the list and select a font size. Or, click on **Format**, then **Font**. Select the **Font** tab. Scroll down the list of font sizes, pick the one you want, then click **OK**.

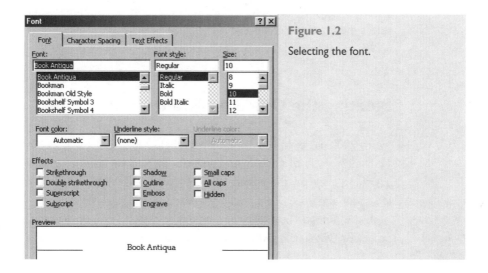

Figure 1.2

Selecting the font.

Figure 1.3

Selecting animation effects.

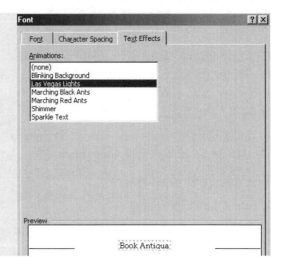

Also under **Format**, **Font**, you will see the **Character Spacing** tab. This lets you change the spacing of letters within a word, their distance from the baseline, and their scale.

Under the **Text Effects** tab, you will find a list of options for animating letters. For example, the **Las Vegas Lights** effect surrounds each word with stars and flashing dots (Fig. 1.3).

To change other settings before typing, open the **Tools** menu and select the **Options** command.

We will discuss the important options later.

Meeting the Office Assistants

Word 2000 has eight assistants that can help you.

Their role is to answer any questions you may have. To call an assistant, click on the speech bubble containing a question mark, located in the upper right corner of your screen (Fig. 1.4).

In the dialogue box that appears, either click on one of the bullet points, or type in a keyword and click on **Search**.

A Help window will be displayed, which will hopefully contain the information required.

If you wish to change the assistant or some of the options, while the assistant is open, click on **Options**.

The **Gallery** tab (Fig. 1.5) introduces you to Clippit, the paper clip, and the other Office Assistants.

Click on **Next** for a presentation of all the Office Assistants.

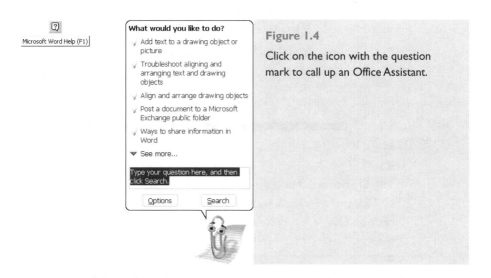

Figure 1.4

Click on the icon with the question mark to call up an Office Assistant.

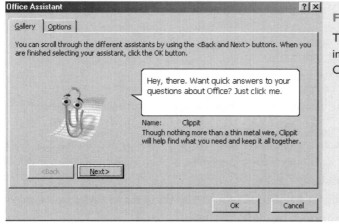

Figure 1.5

The Gallery tab introduces you to the Office Assistants.

Figure 1.6

Making choices in the Options tab.

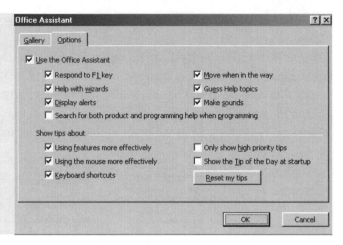

Figure 1.7

The Title bar.

Minimize   Close

Restore/
Maximize

The **Options** tab offers a series of check boxes (Fig. 1.6).

Tick the selections that best suit your personal requirements and click on **OK**.

> The Assistant is common to all Office applications. Any changes you make to it in Word will also apply in Excel or PowerPoint (and vice versa).

Viewing the screen

Before starting work, familiarise yourself with the screen layout.

The Title bar

The Title bar (Fig. 1.7) is located at the top of the Word window.

On the left-hand side, it displays the Word icon, the name of the current document, and the name of the application (Microsoft Word). Clicking on the icon opens a pull-down menu with the following options: Restore, Move, Size, Minimize, Maximize and Close.

On the right-hand side, it shows three icons to minimise, maximise/restore or close the window.

- **To minimise a window**. Click on the **Minimize** button on the right of the Title bar. Alternatively, click on the **Word** icon on the left of the Title bar and select **Minimize**. This takes the window off the desktop and puts it as an entry on the Taskbar at the bottom of your screen.

- **To maximise a window**. Click on the **Maximize** button on the right of the Title bar. Alternatively, click on the **Word** icon on the left of the Title bar and select **Maximize**. This makes the Word application window fill the entire desktop. The **Maximize** button on the right of the Title bar changes name and appearance to become a **Restore** button.

- **To restore a window**. After minimising or maximising a window, you can restore it to its previous size and position on the screen as follows:

  - **After maximising**. Click on the **Restore** button on the right of the Title bar. Alternatively, click on the **Word** icon on the left of the Title bar and select **Restore**.

  - **After minimising**. Click on the window's entry in the **Task bar** at the bottom of your screen.

> *Before moving or resizing a window, you can click on the Word icon on the left of the Title bar and select* **Move** *or* **Size**. *This changes the mouse pointer to a four-directional arrow, which, when clicked outside a corner, border or the Title bar, has no effect on the document.*

- **To switch between windows**. You can have several Word windows open simultaneously. To switch from one to the other, click on the corresponding entry in the Taskbar at the bottom of your screen. Alternatively, you can switch from one to another by pressing **Ctrl+F6**.

- **To move a window**. Click anywhere in the Title bar, then keeping the left mouse button pressed, drag the window to a different position on the screen.

- **To resize a window**. Position the mouse pointer on one of the borders or corners of the window until it changes into a bidirectional horizontal, vertical or diagonal arrow. Keeping the left mouse button depressed, drag it to obtain the desired window size.

- **To close a window**. Click on the **Close** icon on the right of the Title bar. Alternatively, click on the **Word** icon on the left of the Title bar and select **Close**.

The Menu bar

The Menu bar (Fig. 1.8) is located below the Title bar. We will meet most of its menus later.

The Status bar

The Status bar (Fig. 1.9) is located at the bottom of the applications window and displays various current parameter values:

- *Page number*. The number of the page shown, based on the page numbers you gave the document, if any.
- *Sec number*. The section number of the page shown.
- *Number/number*. The page number and the total number of pages based on the physical page count in the document.
- *At number*. The distance from the top of the page to your insertion point. No measurement is displayed if the insertion point is not in the window.
- *Ln number*. The line of text where the insertion point is located. No measurement is displayed if the insertion point is not in the window.
- *Col number*. The distance, in number of characters, from the left margin to the insertion point. No measurement is displayed if the insertion point is not in the window.

Figure 1.8
The Menu bar.

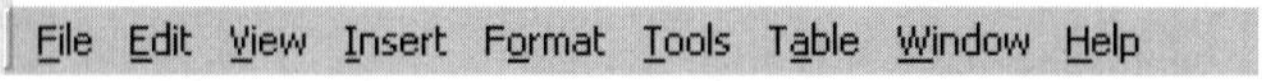

File Edit View Insert Format Tools Table Window Help

Figure 1.9
The Status bar.

Page 1   Sec 1   1/1   At 2.5cm Ln 1   Col 1

The toolbars

The toolbars (Fig. 1.10) are located below the Menu bar.

To customise your toolbars:

1 Open the **Tools** menu.

2 Select **Customize** (Fig. 1.11).

3 Click on the **Commands** tab.

4 Select a command category.

5 Scroll through the commands in the selected category.

6 Click on the ones you want to add, and drag them to your toolbar.

For each icon there is a corresponding explanatory ScreenTip. ScreenTips can be deactivated:

1 Open the **View** menu.

2 Select **Toolbars**.

Figure 1.10

The toolbars.

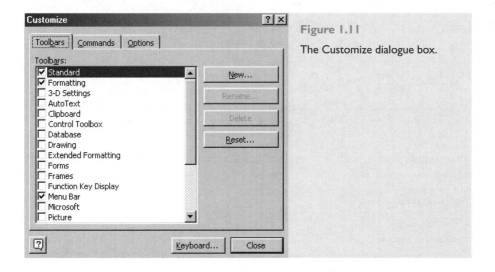

Figure 1.11

The Customize dialogue box.

1: Discovering the software

3 Select **Customize**.

4 Click on the **Options** tab (Fig. 1.12).

5 Clear the **Show ScreenTips on toolbars** check box.

The ruler

The ruler (Fig. 1.13) is displayed differently according to the viewing mode and the current location of the insertion point (normal text, columns or table).

In Normal and Print Layout views, the ruler shows the indent markers and tab stops. The grey portions of the ruler represent the page margins. The current type of tabulation is displayed at the extreme left. Click on this button to change the type of tab stop:

● **Left tab.** Text aligns to the left of the tab stop.

● **Center tab.** Text is centred on the tab stop.

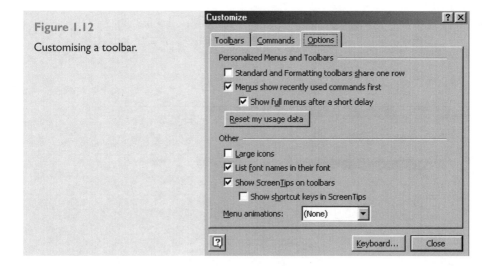

Figure 1.12

Customising a toolbar.

Figure 1.13

The ruler shows the current tab stops.

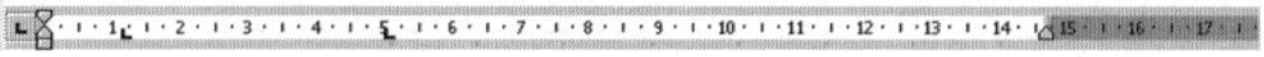

- **Right tab.** Text aligns to the right of the tab stop.
- **Decimal tab.** Numbers align on the decimal point.

Click the ruler where you want to set a tab stop. If necessary, drag the tab stop to position it where you want it. To clear a tab stop, drag it from the ruler.

When the insertion point is in a table, the ruler shows the column markers, which you can click and drag to change column widths. Indent markers are shown for the currently active column.

The scroll bars

There are two scroll bars: one horizontal, at the bottom of the screen (Fig. 1.14), and one vertical, on the right of the screen (Fig. 1.15).

To scroll up one line, click the up scroll arrow. To scroll down one line, click the down scroll arrow.

Figure 1.14

The cursor is pointing to the horizontal scroll bar.

Figure 1.15

The cursor is pointing to the vertical scroll bar.

To scroll up one screen, click above the scroll box. To scroll down one screen, click below the scroll box.

To scroll to a specific page, drag the scroll box.

To move left and right in the text, click the left or right scroll arrow, or drag the scroll box of the horizontal scroll bar.

The cursor

The cursor is one of the most important working tools. It is a visual representation of the mouse on the screen. It can take different forms according to its current operation and environment.

The Text cursor lets you set the insertion point anywhere in the text. It is shaped like an I (Fig. 1.16). Click in any desired location to set the insertion point. Select text by keeping the left-hand mouse button pressed, and dragging the cursor over the text. The text appears highlighted (white letters on a black background).

To use the drag-and-drop function:

1 Select the word to be moved.
2 Keep the mouse button depressed.
3 Drag the word you wish to move. The cursor changes into a white arrow at the centre of a small grey rectangle (Fig. 1.17).

In Print Preview view, the cursor becomes a magnifying glass (Fig. 1.18). You can use this to enlarge the screen. Click the text to be enlarged, and you will see exactly how the printed page will appear.

Figure 1.16
The text insertion point.

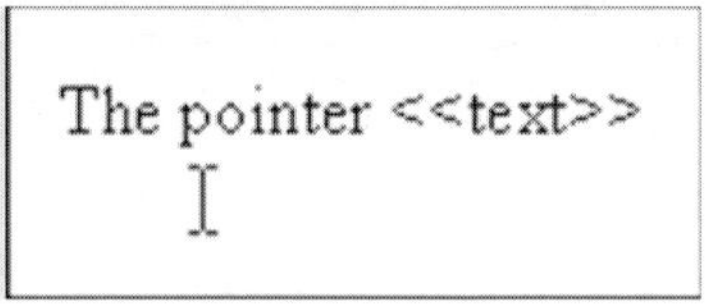

Figure 1.17
The drag-and-drop cursor.

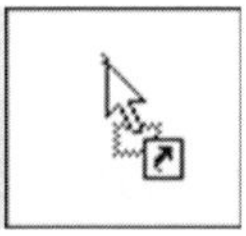

Figure 1.18
The magnifying glass cursor.

Figure 1.19
The resizing cursor.

Figure 1.20
The outline cursor.

Figure 1.21
The Help pointer.

The resizing cursor moves the margins in Print Preview mode. It takes the form of a double-pointed arrow when placed on the ruler (Fig. 1.19).

The outline cursor can move elements in Outline view. It is a cross with four arrowheads (Fig. 1.20). Click on the cross located to the left of the text, then move the highlighted section.

The Help pointer looks like the normal cursor, with a question mark (Fig. 1.21). You can obtain it by Clicking **Help**, **What's This?**

Move the Help pointer to an area of the screen you would like to have explained, and click. An explanation then appears.

To get rid of the Help pointer, click again on **Help**, **What's This?**

Dialogue boxes

Dialogue boxes are designed to give you information on a given subject. To use them, you will need to understand the following terms:

- **Tabs**. Arranged like tabbed cards in an index.
- **Radio buttons**. Allow an option to be selected.
- **Check boxes**. Activated by a simple click with the left mouse button.
- **Text boxes**. Use these to enter text or numerical data.
- **Scroll lists**. Present lists of options for you to choose from.
- **Counters**. Small boxes with arrows for raising or lowering a numerical value.
- **Command buttons**. Allow commands to be validated or cancelled.
- **Closure box**. A button marked by a multiplication sign, located at the top right-hand corner of each box. Clicking one closes that particular active dialogue.

2

Creating a document

- Starting the easy way
- Writing a paragraph
- Viewing modes
- Navigating within the text
- Editing text
- Spelling and grammar
- Multiple insertions
- Saving your work

Starting the easy way

When Word 2000 starts up, the screen is ready for use. Any characters typed will appear immediately on the screen.

Insertion point and end marker

Two reference markers guide you when you start writing. A blinking vertical line about half a centimetre long marks the place where the next letter will be inserted; this is called the insertion point. As you type, it moves to the right.

The second reference marker is a fixed horizontal line, about the same length as the insertion point. This line is always positioned at the beginning of the last line of the text. When you type several lines of text, it moves down.

Click and Type

The new Click and Type tool is designed to make certain tasks easier to perform. For example, unlike in other versions of Word, you can now begin typing anywhere on the page. To do this, the screen must be in **Print Layout** view (click **View**, **Print Layout**). Click and Type is not available when working in multiple columns.

In Click and Type mode, the cursor takes a form adapted to its position (see the Help windows in Fig. 2.1). When you insert into an already typed location, Click and Type adopts the style of the current paragraph.

Giving the text a heading

Type in a heading for your document. As you type, the insertion point moves to the right.

After writing the title, jump several lines by pressing **Enter** a few times.

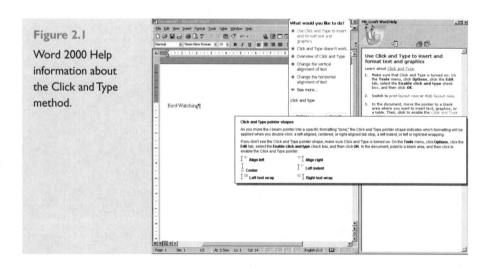

Figure 2.1

Word 2000 Help information about the Click and Type method.

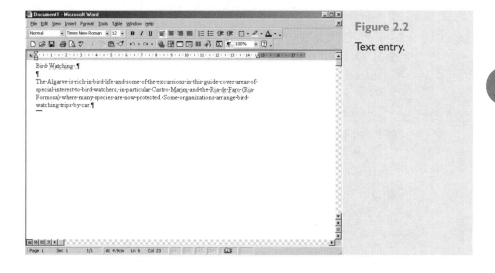

Figure 2.2

Text entry.

The horizontal end-of-text marker moves downwards. You have just introduced some line breaks by pressing the Enter key.

Writing a paragraph

To write the first paragraph, it is necessary to move the insertion point back upwards. To do this, press the up arrow key. The insertion point moves up. Position it two lines below the heading.

You can now type in the whole paragraph (Fig. 2.2). Your text will not have a very finished look, but we will take care of that later.

This is the quickest and most effective way to proceed. For now, be content to type in text as you go.

Viewing modes

Normal mode is the best viewing mode for simple typing.

To change the way in which you display your text, click **View** on the Menu bar. A pull-down menu appears, with a range of options and commands:

- **Normal.** The default document view for the majority of word-processing jobs (Fig. 2.3).

- **Web Layout.** Ideal for displaying and reading documents on screen. In this mode, Word 2000 displays in the same manner as Windows Explorer, which gives quick access to different parts of your document.

- **Print Layout.** Shows how your page will look when printed. This mode makes heavy demands on memory and can slow document scrolling.

- **Outline.** Allows you to work on the document structure. This is the mode you should use for organising and developing the document contents. Outline mode is complex and is not suited to simple preliminary work.

+info

The rulers allow you to locate objects, and to change paragraph indents, margins and other layout parameters.

Viewing mode selection buttons

An alternative way to switch between viewing modes is to use the four selection buttons located at the bottom left corner of the screen, directly above the Status bar (Fig. 2.4).

Figure 2.3

Normal mode is the best mode for straightforward typing.

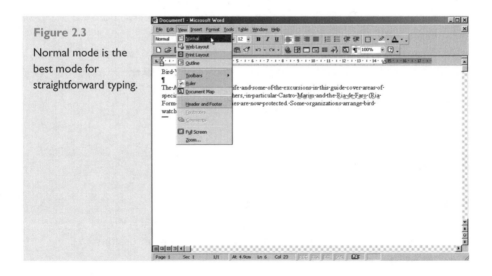

Using Word

For this exercise, choose Print Layout view. The two rulers serve as points of reference and allow margins to be set (you will learn how later) (Fig. 2.5).

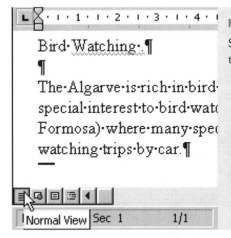

Figure 2.4

Selection buttons for the viewing modes are at the bottom of the screen.

Figure 2.5

The Print Layout view displays two rulers.

Navigating within the text

Moving

Moving is carried out using the mouse or the keyboard. To move the insertion point with the mouse, simply click at the point where you want the insertion point to go.

Alternatively, use the following keyboard shortcuts:

←	One character to the left.
→	One character to the right.
↑	One line up.
↓	One line down.
Ctrl + →	One word to the right.
Ctrl + ←	One word to the left.

For the following moves, the digits must be typed on the numeric keypad.

⇧ + 7	Move to the start of the line.
⇧ + 1	Move to the end of the line.
⇧ + 3	Move one window depth down.
⇧ + 9	Move one window depth up.
Ctrl + alt + pg↓	Move one page down.
Ctrl + alt + pg↑	Move one page up.
Ctrl + 7	Move to the start of the document.
Ctrl + 1	Move to the end of the document.

Scrolling

Scrolling is carried out using the mouse. To scroll the screen up and down, click with the mouse on the up or down black arrows located at the extreme right of your screen.

To scroll by specific item, click on the Browse button located at the bottom of the vertical scroll bar between the two double arrow buttons (Fig. 2.6). A mini-screen appears containing 12 boxes with the options shown in Fig. 2.7.

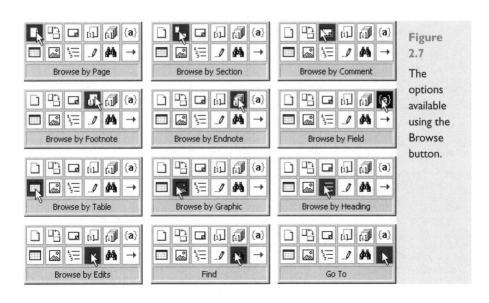

Figure 2.6
The vertical scroll bar with the Browse button.

Select Browse Object (Alt+Ctrl+Home)

Browse by Page	Browse by Section	Browse by Comment
Browse by Footnote	Browse by Endnote	Browse by Field
Browse by Table	Browse by Graphic	Browse by Heading
Browse by Edits	Find	Go To

Figure 2.7

The options available using the Browse button.

Click on the option you require, then use the double arrow buttons to move up or down.

A useful function available in all views shows the page numbers as you scroll. Click on the vertical scroll box to show the current page number. As you move the scroll box up or down, the page number will change.

Editing text

The clipboard

The clipboard lets you store bits of documents, whole documents, or pictures. You can restore them later elsewhere in the document or in another application.

The Word 2000 clipboard can hold 12 different items for an indefinite period.

Cut-and-paste

There are two ways of moving text: cut-and-paste or copy-and-paste, and drag-and-drop.

Cut-and-paste means cutting out the selected text (which is then transferred to the clipboard) for insertion into a different location of the document. The 'cut' action can be effected via the keyboard using the key combination **Ctrl+X**. Alternatively:

1 Select the text you want to cut by double-clicking on it.

2 Click on **Edit** in the menu bar.

3 Click on **Cut**. The text then disappears from the screen.

4 Using the mouse, select your insertion point.

5 Click on **Edit** again.

6 Click on **Paste** (Fig. 2.8). The text is inserted at your chosen location.

You can also use the **Shift+Insert** keyboard shortcut to paste the text at the new location.

Copy-and-paste

To copy a piece of text:

1 Select the text to be copied.

2 Open the **Edit** menu.

3 Select **Copy**.

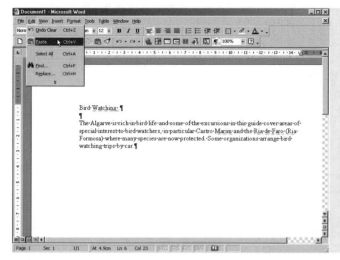

Figure 2.8

Pasting using the Edit menu.

4 Place the insertion point at the desired location.

5 Click on **Paste**.

Drag-and-drop

To relocate text using the drag-and-drop method:

1 Select the text to be moved.

2 Position the cursor within the selection and click, keeping the mouse button depressed until the cursor takes the form of an arrow, the head pointing up to the left.

3 Still keeping the button depressed, drag the text to its new location. During the move, the cursor takes the form of a small rectangle, below the arrow.

4 At the new location, release the mouse button. The selected text is inserted and everything returns to normal.

Undoing and redoing commands

To undo an action, select **Edit**, **Undo**.

You can also change your mind and reverse an Undo change by selecting **Edit**, **Redo**.

Figure 2.9

The Undo button.

Another way of undoing an action is to use the **Ctrl** (Control) key, and keep it depressed while pressing the **Z** key. The **Ctrl+Z** key combination reverses the last action.

Likewise, the **Ctrl+Y** combination allows you to redo an action. Finally, there are two buttons on the toolbar that let you undo or redo actions (Fig. 2.9).

Spelling and grammar

To check your spelling and grammar:

1 Open the **Tools** menu.

2 Click on **Spelling and Grammar**. Alternatively, click on the ABC button, which is usually found next to the Print Preview button (magnifying glass motif) on the Standard toolbar.

To correct a spelling mistake, just follow the suggested corrections that appear. You can accept suggestions, ignore them, or add new words to the dictionary. These will be recognised in future just like the initial dictionary entries.

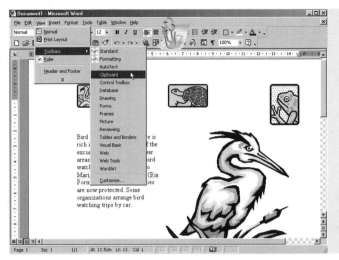

Figure 2.10

To use the new clipboard, its toolbar must be displayed.

The grammar checker offers grammatical corrections presented clearly and simply. Again, you can ignore the suggestion, or make the recommended correction.

Multiple insertions

Apart from the traditional copy-and-paste commands, Word 2000 offers a clipboard that can hold up to 12 different items. Unfortunately, the contents of the cache cannot be viewed, which limits its utilisation since you have to remember the contents of each item. When the content is text, the help balloon displays the start of the text. For pictures, the Item 1, Item 2 ... label is shown.

To use the clipboard, click on **View Toolbars**, then select **Clipboard** (Fig. 2.10).

Saving your work

Once you have entered and corrected your text, you should save it. Let's assume you want to save it on the C drive. In this case, you have to create a directory on the C disk.

25

1 Access Windows Explorer by clicking on **Start**, **Programs**, **Windows Explorer** (Fig. 2.11).

2 Select the C drive (Fig. 2.12).

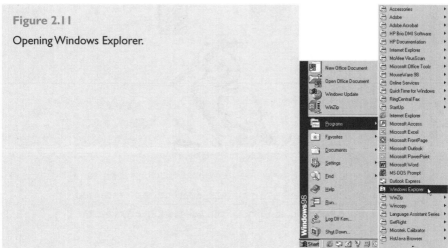

Figure 2.11

Opening Windows Explorer.

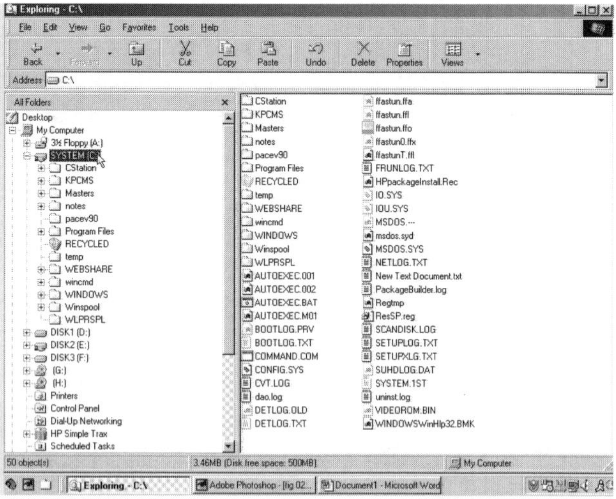

Figure 2.12

Selecting the C drive.

Using Word

To choose a directory:

1 After selecting the C drive, open the **File** menu.

2 Select **New**.

3 Select the **Folder** option (Fig. 2.13).

Now enter a name for your folder in the name box.

Similarly, you can create subdirectories of the main directory.

It is recommended that you save your work every five or ten minutes. You can set your PC to automatically save every few minutes. In
Word, click on **Tools**, **Options**. Click on the **Save** tab. Tick the
Save Auto Recover info every box, and specify the save time
interval. Click **OK**.

Giving your file a name

Up to now your file has probably had the default name Document1.

To give it a more descriptive name:

1 Open the **File** menu.

2 Select **Save As**.

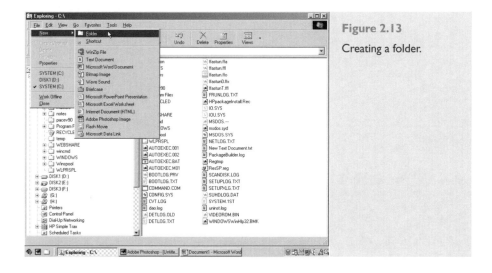

Figure 2.13
Creating a folder.

3 In the **File name** box at the bottom of the dialogue box, enter your chosen name. Word 2000 suggests you save the file as a Word document. However, several other formats are available, allowing you to share files with other users (Macintosh, for example). To select a different format, click on the scrolled list in the **Save as type** box.

3

Formatting a page

- Aligning text
- Setting indents
- Widows and orphans
- Borders and shading
- Lists
- Selecting a font
- Adding emphasis
- Setting margins
- Headers and footers
- Displaying page numbers
- Applying the date and time

Formatting a page consists of applying normal methods of presentation but adding a personal touch.

Aligning text

Text can be left-aligned, right-aligned, centred or justified. Left-aligned is the Word 2000 default alignment. For each form of alignment there is a button on the Formatting toolbar (Fig. 3.1).

Figure 3.1
The Align Left, Center, Align Right and Justify buttons.

- **Left-aligned** text is aligned down the left margin, but is uneven, or ragged, at the right margin.
- **Right-aligned** text is flush with the right margin and uneven at the left margin.
- **Centred** text is set evenly between the two margins.
- **Justified** text is aligned with both margins.

> Do not confuse the setting of paragraph indents with the definition of the left or right margins. Paragraph indents are measured from the margin lines, not from the paper edges. Margin settings define the blank spaces left around the text.

Setting indents

You can set indents easily using the ruler. The ruler carries indent markers in the shape of small triangles, which you can slide left or right.

Modifying the first line indent

On the graduated ruler, the small triangle pointing downwards is the indent marker for the first line of a paragraph. The indent can be to the left (negative indent) or the right (positive indent) (Fig. 3.2).

Changing the paragraph indent

On the graduated ruler, the small triangle pointing upwards is the left paragraph indent marker. Move it to set your paragraph indent (Fig. 3.3).

Alternatively, select **Format**, **Paragraph**, and change the settings in the **Indents and Spacing** tab (Fig. 3.4).

To apply an alignment to the whole of the text, select the whole text with **Ctrl+A**, or by clicking on **Edit**, **Select All**. Then apply the relevant alignment.

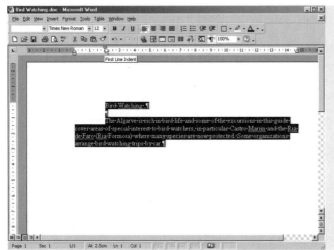

Figure 3.2

Text with an indented
first paragraph line.

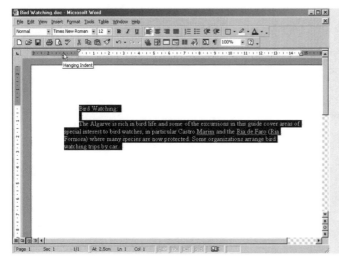

Figure 3.3

Text with a left
paragraph indent.

Widows and orphans

In printing, a widow is the last line of a paragraph appearing as the
first line on a new page.

An orphan is the first line of a new paragraph appearing at the
foot of a page.

Figure 3.4

The Indents and Spacing tab in the Paragraph dialogue box.

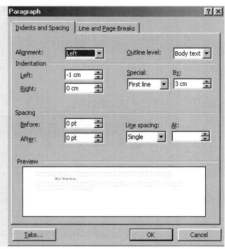

Figure 3.5

The Line and Page Breaks tab in the Paragraph dialogue box.

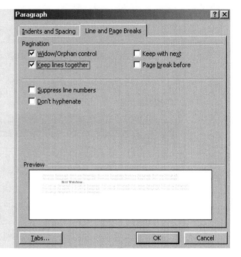

The widow/orphan control option in Word makes reading the text a more fluid process. Go to **Format**, **Paragraph**, and click on the **Line and Page Breaks** tab (Fig. 3.5). Tick the **Widow/Orphan control** box.

Ticking the **Keep lines together** box means that lines in a paragraph will not be separated at all.

Ticking the **Keep with next** box prohibits a page break directly after a paragraph. This is a very useful function if, for example, you want to keep a chart and its caption together.

Borders and shading

You can place borders around pages, phrases, words, pictures and tables, and create basic frames in any colour.

Borders

To apply a border to a piece of text, select the text, then click on **Format**, **Borders and Shading**.
There are different types of border:

Box Shadow

3-D Custom

Borders can be continuous or dotted.

Word 2000 offers 150 new borders. Amongst them are several borders in 3D and frames intended for the publication of brochures or small papers.

Shading

You can use shading to add emphasis to a piece of text:

1 Select the text you want to shade.

2 Open the **Format** menu, then select **Borders and Shading**.

3 Click on the **Shading** tab.

4 Select a colour or a shade of grey.

5 Click **OK**.

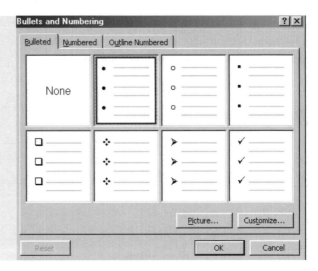

Figure 3.6

The Bulleted tab of the Bullets and Numbering dialogue box.

Lists

To create a bulleted list, type in the list, pressing **Enter** after each entry. Select the list. Then click on the **Bullets** button on the toolbar. For a numbered list, click on the **Numbering** button instead of the Bullets button.

To change the appearance of the bullet symbol in a list:

1 Open the **Format** menu.

2 Click on **Bullets and Numbering**.

3 Select the **Bulleted** tab (Fig. 3.6).

4 Click on the bullets you want to use and click **OK**.

To change the numbering of a list, select the **Numbered** tab instead of the Bulleted tab.

Selecting a font

TrueType fonts are displayed exactly as they will print. They can be printed by all printers. The TrueType label is abbreviated to TT at the side of each font name.

34

The default font in Word is Times New Roman. It is used in new documents created from the active normal template.

To select a font before typing:

1 Open the **Format** menu.

2 Click on **Font**.

3 Select the **Font** tab.

4 Scroll the list of fonts, and click on the one that suits you.

5 Confirm with the **OK** button.

To change the font of text that has been written, select your text, then follow the procedure above. Alternatively, use the **Font** box on the toolbar.

To change the font size, click on the **Font Size** arrow on the Formatting toolbar, and click on a new point size.

Adding emphasis

To emphasise text:

1 Select the text you want to emphasise.

2 Open the **Format** menu.

3 Select **Font**.

4 Click on the **Font** tab.

5 In the **Font style** box, choose Regular, Italic, Bold, or Bold Italic.

6 Click **OK**.

Font effects

There are also some other ways of enriching text:

1 Select the text you are enriching.

2 Open the **Format** menu.

3 Click on **Font**.

4 Choose the **Font** tab.

5 In the **Effects** area, tick the effects you want.

6 Click **OK**.

The options available are:

- **Strikethrough**. Draws a line through the selected text.
- **Double strikethrough**. Draws a double line through the selected text.
- **Shadow**. Adds a shadow behind the selected text.
- **Outline**. Displays the inner and outer borders of each character.
- **Emboss**. Makes selected text appear as if it is raised off the page.
- **Engrave**. Makes selected text appear as though printed or pressed into the page.
- **Small caps**. Changes lower-case letters into small-size capitals. Does not affect numbers, punctuation, non-alphabetic characters or upper-case letters.

The Highlight option can be used to emphasise text. Click on the Highlight button (marker icon) in the Formatting toolbar, then select the text or object to highlight. When finished, click again on the button to deselect it. To change the marker colour, click on the drop-down arrow beside the Highlight button.

Further options include **Superscript** and **Subscript** (as used, for example, in m^2 and H_2O), **All caps** and **Hidden**.

Dropped capitals

To insert a dropped capital at the start of your text (Fig. 3.7):

1 Select the first letter of your paragraph.

2 Open the **Format** menu.

3 Select **Drop Cap**.

4 Click on **Dropped** (Fig. 3.8).

5 Confirm with **OK**.

Figure 3.7

A dropped capital
can improve the
appearance of
your text.

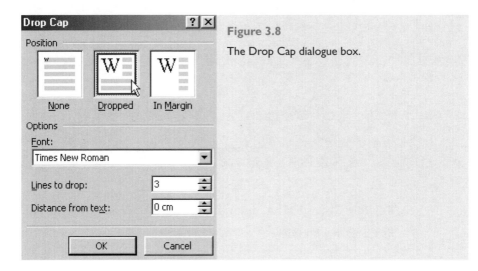

Figure 3.8

The Drop Cap dialogue box.

Case

To change the case of a character or piece of text:

1 Select the text.

2 Open the **Format** menu.

3 Select **Change Case**.

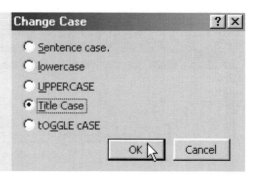

Figure 3.9

The Change Case dialogue box.

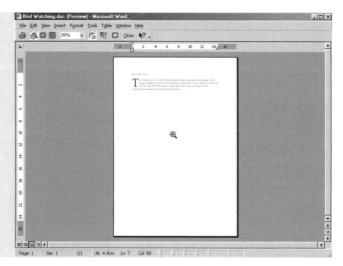

Figure 3.10

Print Preview and the magnifying glass cursor.

4 In the **Change Case** dialogue box, tick the relevant box (Fig. 3.9).

5 Confirm with **OK**.

Setting margins

Preview your text to get an idea of what it will look like when printed:

1 Open the **View** menu.

2 Select **Print Preview** (Fig. 3.10).

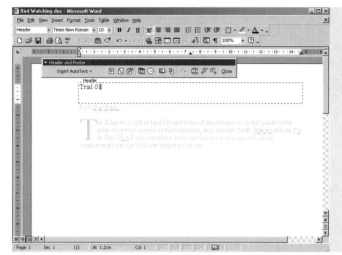

Figure 3.11

Entering text in the
Header box of
the Header and
Footer option.

You can also click on the toolbar button representing a sheet of paper and a magnifying glass.

The Print Preview allows you to see whether the text fits on the page. To change the top margin:

1 Slide the cursor over the top margin limit on the ruler at the left of the screen.

2 The cursor changes to a double-headed arrow. Slide this, keeping the left mouse button depressed, to set the size of the top margin.

You can also set the margins in Page Layout view (**View**, **Page Layout**) in the same way.

Headers and footers

To add headers and footers to your document:

1 Open the **View** menu.

2 Select **Header and Footer**. A text zone labelled Header appears.

3 Enter the header text in the text box (Fig. 3.11).

Figure 3.12

The Switch Between Header and Footer button.

Switch Between Header and Footer

4 Now click on the **Switch Between Header and Footer** button (Fig. 3.12).

5 The Footer area then appears, where you can enter, for example, page numbers, the date, time, etc.

Displaying page numbers

Page numbers are updated automatically when you add or remove pages.

To display the current page number with the total number of pages:

1 Open the **View** menu.

2 Click on **Header and Footer**.

3 Click on the **Switch Between Header and Footer** button to go to the **Footer** area.

4 Open the **Insert AutoText** drop-down list on the **Header and Footer** toolbar.

5 Select the **Page X** of **Y** option (Fig. 3.13).

6 You can format this text in the normal ways.

Applying the date and time

This function allows the last revision date of the document to be shown.

1 Open the **View** menu.

2 Click on the **Header and Footer** option.

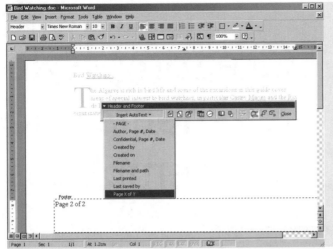

Figure 3.13

Inserting page
numbers.

Figure 3.14

Inserting the time
automatically.

3 Switch from the header to the footer area.

4 Click on the **Insert Time** button (Fig. 3.14). The system time is
   inserted automatically.

5 Click on the **Insert Date** button (two calendar pages icon). The
   system date is inserted automatically.

4

Creating style sheets and templates

- Creating a style sheet
- Modifying a style sheet
- Printing a style sheet
- Choosing a template
- Creating a template
- Adding macros

 Style sheets let you change the formatting of a whole document in a few easy steps.

A style sheet comprises a collection of styles presented in a scrolled list box. A style comprises all the characteristics of a paragraph (indent measurements, alignment, borders, font, etc.). Applying a style to a paragraph automatically endows it with all the characteristics of that style.

Creating a style sheet

To create a style sheet, you must first define each style by giving it form and a name.

Using the toolbar

1 Select the text to be styled.

2 Click on the **Style** box located at the extreme left of the Formatting toolbar. This box contains a scrolled list of style names. By default, you will find Normal, Heading 1, Heading 2, Heading 3, Hyperlink and Default Paragraph Font (Fig. 4.1).

3 In the text box, write the name that you want to give your new style, and press **Enter**.

Using the dialogue box

1 Select the text to which you want to attribute a style.

2 Open the **Format** menu.

3 Select **Style**. The dialogue box (Fig. 4.2) contains the list of styles contained within your document.

4 Click on **New**.

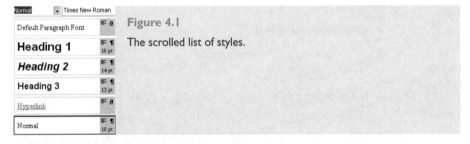

Figure 4.1

The scrolled list of styles.

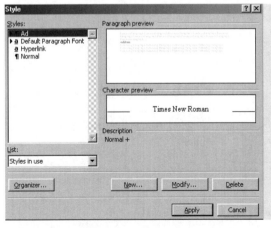

Figure 4.2

The Style dialogue box.

5   In the area entitled **Name**, enter the new name you wish to give to the style. Let's say that it's Signature.

6   The Description area lists the characteristics of the selected paragraph. If you want to change these characteristics, click on **Format** and select **Font**.

7   Choose **Bold**, for example. Click on **OK**.

8   Confirm your formatting choices by clicking on **OK**.

9   If you wish to create additional styles, proceed from step 3 for the other styles.

10 When you have finished, click on either **Apply** to apply and save any changes you have made, or **Cancel** to close the dialogue box without applying your changes.

Modifying a style sheet

To improve or modify a style sheet:

1   Click **Format**, **Style**.

2   Select the style you want to alter.

3   Click **Modify**.

4   In the Modify Style dialogue box (Fig. 4.3), format the style as shown before.

5   Tick the **Add to template** and **Automatically update** boxes.

6   Click **OK**.

7   Select **Apply**.

You will see in the Modify Style dialogue box that some styles are based on others. Modifying the basic style will change those based on it.

Printing a style sheet

To print the style sheet you have just defined:

1   Select the **File** menu.

2   Click on **Print**.

3   In the **Print what?** box, select **Styles** (Fig. 4.4).

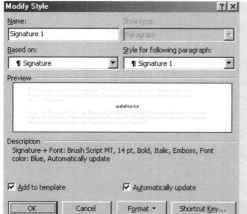

Figure 4.3

The Modify Style dialogue box.

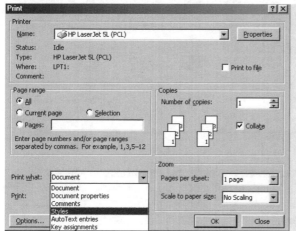

Figure 4.4

Printing styles from the Print dialogue box.

Choosing a template

With style sheets, you can modify a document format by copying styles. Another solution is to use a template.

A template is a document saved in a predefined format. To apply a template to a document:

> When the **Automatically update** button is ticked, the style is updated whenever you modify it, which ensures consistent styling for the various document elements (e.g. the headings). To deactivate this function, select **Format, Style**, select the style concerned, and then click on **Modify**. Untick the **Automatically update** box.

1 Open the **File** menu.

2 Click on **New**.

3 Select the template of your choice.

4 Select the **Create New Document** option (Fig. 4.5).

In the new document that appears, test the different styles on offer.

The standard templates supplied by Microsoft are usually located in the **C:\Program Files\Microsoft Office\Templates** subdirectory (Fig. 4.6). They have the file extension .dot. You can access them all by clicking on the **File, New** command.

Figure 4.5

Selecting the Create New Document option.

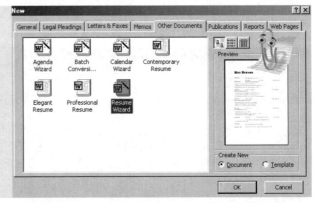

Figure 4.6

The set of Microsoft Office templates.

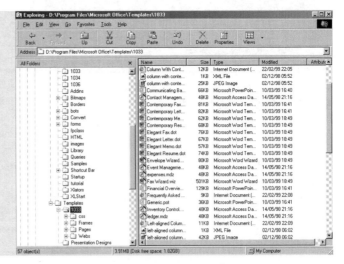

Creating a template

For precisely formatted documents, you can create your own style sheets.

To create a style sheet, proceed as before:

1 Open the **File** menu.

2 Select **New**.

3 Click on the **General** tab.

4 Choose **Blank Document**.

5 Select the **Create New Document** option.

Now create your template.

To save the template so you can re-use it, click on **File**, **Save As**. Give your template a name. In the **Save as type** box, scroll down to **Document Template**. Then save in the usual way.

Adding macros

Templates can be improved by the addition of macros. You can create, for example, a library of signatures, or personalised headers and footers.

1 Activate the WordArt Toolbar by clicking on **View**, **Toolbars**, **WordArt**.

2 Click on **Tools**, **Macro**, **Record New Macro**.

3 Enter a short name, for example 'S1' for your signature.

4 Decide where to store the macro (in Normal.dot or only in the open file).

5 Click on **OK**.

6 On your page, type the text to comprise the macro. Format it in the usual way.

7 When you have finished, click on the **Stop Recording** (square) button.

To insert the text you have recorded, click on **Tools**, **Macro**, **Macros**. Click on the macro you want to run, and click **Run**.

5

Improving the first draft

- Find and Replace
- AutoCorrect
- Finding doubles
- Finding synonyms
- Creating your own dictionary
- AutoText
- Document statistics
- Inserting comments
- Tracking changes

Find and Replace

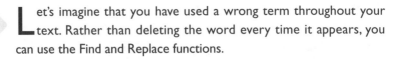

Let's imagine that you have used a wrong term throughout your text. Rather than deleting the word every time it appears, you can use the Find and Replace functions.

1 Open the **Edit** menu.

2 Click on the **Replace** option.

3 Select the **Replace** tab.

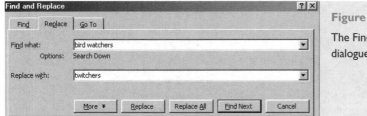

4 Enter the word that you want to delete in the **Find what** box
(Fig. 5.1).

5 Now type in the word you want to replace it with in the **Replace with** box.

6 Confirm the entry by clicking on the **Replace All** button.

If you click **Replace** instead of **Replace All**, the function will show
you, one by one, all occurrences of the word to be replaced – just in
case there is an instance where you don't want to replace it.

AutoCorrect

The AutoCorrect function automatically corrects certain errors as you
type. You can also program it to finish off long words or phrases after
you have typed the first few letters or an abbreviation of the phrase.

Some words are already included in the AutoCorrect list. For
example, if you type in 'yeras', Word takes over and changes it to
'years' (Fig. 5.2).

To add a word or phrase to the AutoCorrect list:

1 Click on **Tools**.

2 Select **AutoCorrect**.

3 In the **Replace** box, type in the word or letters that you want
Word to recognise as an error.

4 In the **With** box, type in the word or phrase that you want to
replace the other word with.

Figure 5.2

Corrections while you type.

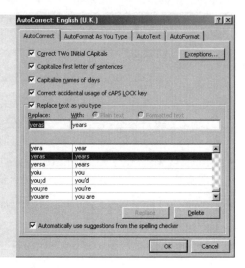

5 Click on **Add** to add the word to the AutoCorrect list.

6 Click on **OK**.

To remove a word or phrase from the list:

1 Click on **Tools**.

2 Select **AutoCorrect**.

3 Click on the relevant phrase in the scroll-down list of corrections.

4 Click on **Delete**.

5 Click on **OK**.

Completing a word automatically

The AutoComplete function saves time when entering certain words. It can add the last letters of the names of days and months, and the last digits of dates.

For example, if you type in 'Octo', the word October appears in a ScreenTip. Press **Enter** to confirm it and the word is completed for you (Fig. 5.3).

Figure 5.3

The word October is completed automatically.

Extra Word

Only one of the marked words is necessary to signal that a noun follows.

• Instead of: <u>The a</u> distance runner must practice every day.
• Consider: A distance runner must practice every day.
• Or consider: The distance runner must practice every day.

• Instead of: <u>The this</u> pie was the best he had ever baked.
• Consider: This pie was the best he had ever baked.
• Or consider: The pie was the best he had ever baked.

Figure 5.4

The spell checker has identified a double occurrence.

Finding doubles

As well as checking for spelling errors, the spell checker finds words repeated twice in a row (Fig. 5.4).

Finding synonyms

To use the thesaurus:

1 Select the word for which you would like a synonym.

2 Open the **Tools** menu.

3 Select the **Language** option.

4 Select **Thesaurus**. A dialogue box offers you synonyms for the word based on a standard dictionary entry. In addition, you are offered the meanings of the word. Select the synonym that you want to replace your original word with.

5 Click on the **Replace** button.

51

Figure 5.5

The Custom Dictionaries dialogue box.

Creating your own dictionary

The spell checker compares the terms in your text with those in its dictionary. It is likely that certain words and expressions that you use do not figure in this dictionary. You can create a personal dictionary that the spell checker will consult for each correction:

1 Open the **Tools** menu.

2 Choose **Options**.

3 Click on the **Spelling and Grammar** tab.

4 Click on the **Dictionaries** button.

5 Press the **New** button in the **Custom Dictionaries** dialogue box (Fig. 5.5).

In the **File name** box, enter a name for your dictionary.

AutoText

The **AutoText** menu lets you insert various lines of text at the click of a button:

1 Open the **Insert** menu.

Figure 5.6 caption area

Figure 5.6

The AutoText menu.

2 Select **AutoText**. The AutoText menu lists a choice of items to insert, e.g. standard greetings or closures, mailing instructions, and so on (Fig. 5.6).

3 Click on the expression you want to insert, and it will be added automatically.

Document statistics

Sometimes, it is useful to know the number of words, lines or even characters in a document.

1 Select either the whole document (**Ctrl+A**) or a particular section of text to be checked.

2 Open the **File** menu.

3 Select the **Properties** option.

4 Click on the **Statistics** tab (Fig. 5.7).

> **+info**
>
> The **Word Count** option on the **Tools** menu counts the number of pages, words, characters, paragraphs and lines contained in your document. Punctuation marks and special characters are included.

Figure 5.7

Extracting document statistics.

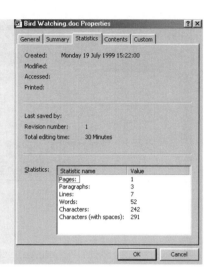

Inserting comments

To insert comments relating to your text:

1 Open the **Insert** menu.

2 Click on the **Comment** option.

3 Select the word or group of words where you wish to add a comment.

4 In the text input zone at the bottom of the screen, enter the comment that you wish to attach to the word (Fig. 5.8).

These comments won't appear in the final document when you print it.

Tracking changes

Word 2000 allows you to track any changes that you make to a document:

1 Open the **Tools** menu.

2 Select the **Track Changes** option.

3 Choose **Highlight Changes**.

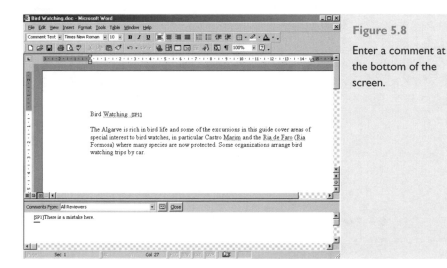

Figure 5.8

Enter a comment at the bottom of the screen.

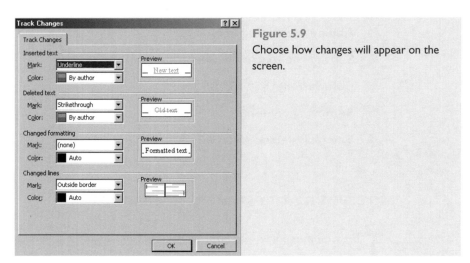

Figure 5.9

Choose how changes will appear on the screen.

4 Tick the **Highlight changes on screen** box.

5 Click on **Options** to customise the way in which the changes will appear on your screen (Fig. 5.9).

6

Working with columns

- Presenting a document in columns
- Creating a heading across several columns
- Changing the number of columns
- Adding separating lines
- Setting the spacing between columns
- Column length
- Removing columns
- The Newsletter Wizard

Presenting a document in columns

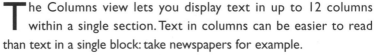

The Columns view lets you display text in up to 12 columns within a single section. Text in columns can be easier to read than text in a single block: take newspapers for example.

To present text in columns:

1 First type in all of the text.

2 Place the cursor at the beginning of the section you want to set in columns.

3 Open the **Insert** menu.

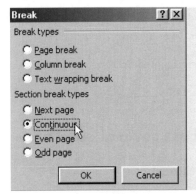

Figure 6.1
The Break dialogue box.

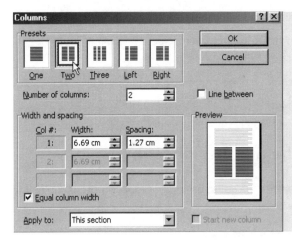

Figure 6.2
In the Columns dialogue box,
select the number of columns.

4 Select the **Break** option.

5 Select the **Continuous** button (Fig. 6.1).

6 Place the cursor somewhere in the section to be set in columns.

7 Open the **Format** menu.

8 Select the **Columns** option.

9 Select the number of columns you want. Then click **OK** (Fig. 6.2).

10 If you are not already in Page Layout view, click on **View, Page Layout**.

11 Place the cursor at the end of the first column.

12 Select **Insert, Break, Column break**.

Your document is now set in two columns. You can go ahead and format it using justification and so on.

Creating a heading across several columns

To create a heading across several columns:

1 If your text is not yet set in columns, create the columns.

2 In **Page Layout** view, select the text for the heading.

3 Click on **Format Columns**. Then select one column in the **Columns** dialogue box.

4 To centre the title over the column, keeping the title selected, click on the **Center** tab in the formatting toolbar.

Changing the number of columns

To change the number of columns in your document, perform the following:

1 Change to **Print Layout** view.

2 Select the section you want to change.

3 Open the **Format** menu.

4 Click on the **Columns** option.

5 Select the number of columns you want.

Adding separating lines

To add separating lines between your columns, change to Print Layout view.

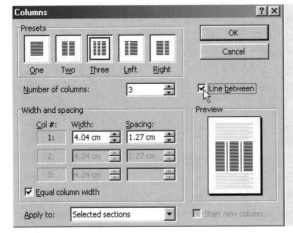

Figure 6.3

Adding lines between columns.

1 Click in the section to be modified.

2 Open the **Format** menu.

3 Select the **Columns** option.

4 Tick the **Line between** check box (Fig. 6.3).

Setting the spacing between columns

By default, the spacing between columns is 1.27 cm. You can change this spacing using the ruler or columns dialogue box.

Using the ruler

1 If the ruler is not switched on, open the **View** menu.

2 Select the **Ruler** option. The grey areas of the ruler represent the spacing between the columns.

3 Place your cursor on one of the grey margin limits. It changes into a double-headed arrow.

4 Press and drag the arrow cursors on the ruler to increase or reduce the spacing between the columns. You can move them left or right. If **Equal column width** is activated for a document in the **Columns** dialogue box, changes will apply to both columns.

Figure 6.4

Changing the width and spacing
of the columns.

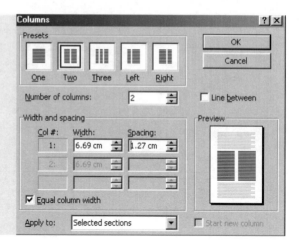

Using the Columns dialogue box

1 Place the insertion point in the section you wish to change.

2 Open the **Format** menu.

3 Select the **Columns** option. The dialogue box is displayed.

4 Use the **Width** and **Spacing** adjustment arrows to change the
   column width and spacing (Fig. 6.4).

Column length

If your text is long, it is important that the columns have the same
length and width throughout. Word 2000 evens up the length of the
columns and aligns them automatically. However, your text may still
contain a widowed or orphaned column. To remedy this:

1 Place the insertion point at the end of the text.

2 Open the **Insert** menu.

3 Select the **Break** option.

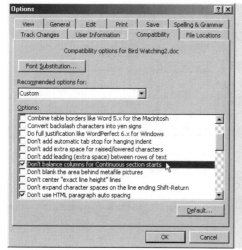

4 Tick the **Continuous** box.

5 Confirm by clicking **OK**.

Your columns will be balanced by the insertion of a section break at
the end of the document.

If your columns are still not balanced, go to **Tools, Options**. Click
the **Compatibility** tab. Make sure the **Don't balance columns
for Continuous section starts** box is deactivated (Fig. 6.5).

Removing columns

To change the column format back to normal text:

1 Place the insertion point in the section you wish to alter.

2 Open the **Format** menu.

3 Select the **Columns** option.

4 Change the column number to one.

Figure 6.6

The Newsletter Wizard asks which style to use for your letter.

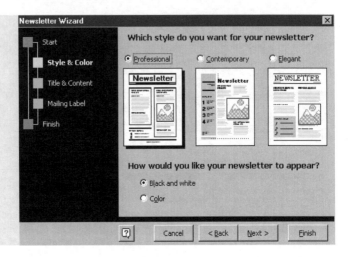

The Newsletter Wizard

The Newsletter Wizard helps you produce a newsletter.

1 Open the **File** menu.

2 Click on **New**.

3 Click the **Publications** tab.

4 Select **Newsletter Wizard** (Fig. 6.6).

5 Let the wizard guide you through the process of creating a newsletter.

7

Illustrating a document

Customising the Drawing toolbar

Word 2000 offers many powerful drawing tools that were previously reserved for specialised graphic illustration software. Useful tools include:

- **Edit Wrap Points**. Lets you run text around part of an image.
- **Set Transparent Color**. Sets the colour you wish to make transparent. You can use transparent areas to integrate a picture on your page, e.g. when you have a picture of a person and don't want the background colour to be visible.
- **Crop**. Lets you reframe a picture.
- **More/Less Brightness/Contrast**. Four tools to adjust the colours. Over- or underexposed photos can now be corrected quickly.
- **Depth**. Adjusts the depth of 3D objects.
- **Shadow Settings**. A set of tools to switch the shadow effect on and off, attribute a colour to the shadow, and move the shadow stepwise up/down/left/right.
- **Rotate or Flip**. A set of tools for rotating and flipping objects.

To view the Drawing toolbar, click on **View**, **Toolbars**. Select the **Drawing** option. To add extra tools to the Drawing toolbar, click on **Tools**, **Customize**. Select the **Commands** tab, then select **Drawing**. Select the tools you want and drag them to the Drawing toolbar.

Inserting a WordArt object

You can create titles and texts in 3D thanks to the WordArt utility:

1 Place your cursor where you wish to insert your title.

2 Open the **Insert** menu.

3 Open the **Picture** submenu.

4 Click on **WordArt**.

5 Double-click the WordArt style of your choice (Fig. 7.1).

6 Enter your title in the Edit WordArt Text dialogue box.

7 Select font and size.

8 Click on **OK**. Your title is then displayed showing the chosen effect.

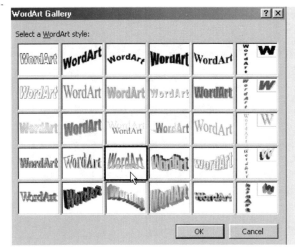

Figure 7.1
Predefined WordArt effects.

Now you can either leave your title as it is or add extra effects.
To rotate the title:

1   First select the title: slide the cursor over the title until it forms a
cross of four arrows; now click once.

2   Click on the **Free Rotate** button in the WordArt toolbar.

3   Place the cursor, which should now be a white arrow in front of a
circular arrow, on one of the green dots ('handles') that appear at
the corners of the title.

4   Keeping the mouse button pressed, drag the handle until the text
is in the right place.

The WordArt Shape option, indicated by the **Abc** icon, lets you
change the title even further.
To apply a WordArt shape:

1   Select title as before.

2   Click on the **WordArt Shape (Abc)** icon.

3   Select a shape (Fig. 7.2).

Figure 7.2

WordArt shapes.

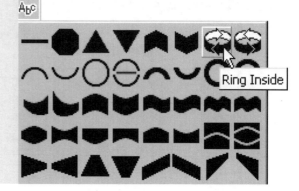

Editing text

The Edit Text button on the WordArt toolbar lets you edit your text at any time, without changing its predefined style.

1 Select the WordArt object as before.

2 Click on the **Edit Text** button on the WordArt toolbar. The **Edit Text** dialogue box appears on the screen. You can change the font, point size and character style, and make the usual kinds of editing changes.

Changing the colour

To change the colours of predefined WordArt objects:

1 Select the WordArt object as usual.

2 Using the **Fill Color** drop-down arrow on the Drawing toolbar, select the colour for your title.

You can also add colour effects using the **Fill Effects** option of the **Fill Color** button.

Spacing

To set the spacing of a WordArt object, click on the **AV** button on the WordArt toolbar. You can set the text characters in your object to be Very Tight, Tight, Normal, Loose, Very Loose, or opt for Custom.

WordArt object parameters

To set the parameters for a WordArt object, click on the **Format WordArt** button on the WordArt toolbar. This opens a dialogue box that lets you change the style of the colours, lines, layout, etc.

Lighting

To change the lighting effects of a WordArt object:

1 Select your object in the usual way.

2 In the Drawings toolbar, click on the **3-D** icon.

3 Click on the **3-D Settings** button to open the 3-D Settings toolbar.

4 Select the **Lighting** icon.

5 Choose the intensity: Bright, Normal or Dim (Fig. 7.3).

6 Set the lighting direction by clicking on the appropriate lighting button.

Figure 7.3

The Bright option in the 3-D Settings Lighting dialogue box.

Adding a shadow

To add a shadow to an object:

1 Select the object.

2 Click on the **Shadow** icon on the Drawing toolbar.

3 Choose the shadow effect you want.

To adjust the position of the shadow or to change its colour, click on the **Shadow Settings** option of the **Shadow** button.

> *You can add a shadow or a 3D effect, but not both at the same time. If you apply a 3D style to a design that already has a shadow, the shadow disappears; and vice versa.*

Inserting AutoShapes

You can enhance your text by adding an AutoShape chosen from the 100 or so offered by Word 2000:

1 Click the **AutoShapes** button on the Drawing toolbar. Or open the **Insert** menu, and select **Picture**, **AutoShapes**.

2 Select the type of shape you want, e.g. **Callouts**.

3 Select the shape, e.g. **Cloud Callout** (Fig. 7.4).

4 Click the cursor where you want to place the shape.

5 Click on the **Text Box** icon in the Drawing toolbar. The cursor changes to a cross: move it to the inside of the shape.

6 Type your text inside the shape.

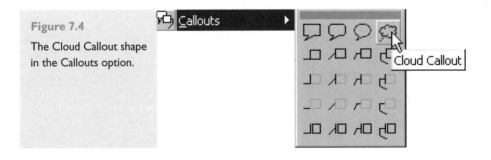

Figure 7.4

The Cloud Callout shape in the Callouts option.

Adding a drawing in front of or behind your text

You can insert a drawing or AutoShape in the same layer as the text, behind the text or in front of the text.

When it is inserted, a drawing will always be in front of the text. To put it behind the text:

1 Select the object or shape.

2 Open the **Draw** menu on the Drawing toolbar.

3 Select **Order**.

4 Click on **Send Behind Text**.

Wrapping text around irregular objects

To wrap text around an irregular shape:

1 Select the object or shape.

2 Open the **Format** menu.

3 Click on **AutoShape**, **Text Box**, **Picture** or **Object**.

4 Select the **Wrapping** tab.

5 Choose the type of wrapping you want.

6 Under **Distance from text**, specify the distance between the text and the box or graphic.

Customising a page border

Word 2000 lets you surround each page with a customised border. To access these borders:

1 Open the **Format** menu.

2 Select **Borders and Shading** (Fig. 7.5).

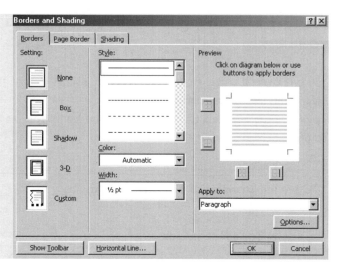

Figure 7.5
Creating a customised border.

To place a border around a paragraph, click anywhere in the paragraph. To place a border around a specific text or a certain word, select it. To enclose only specific edges, click in the Preview section on the side or sides you want.

To specify the exact position of the border in relation to the text:

1 In the Borders and Shading dialogue box, click on the **Options** button.

2 Select the desired options.

8

Creating tables

Creating a table

You can create tables composed of rows and columns which you define. The intersection of a row and a column is called a cell. Inside a cell, you can enter a number, word, phrase, paragraph, chart or picture. Each cell is independent. You can insert your table anywhere in the document, resize it, and add a title, caption, equation or customised borders.

To insert a table into your document:

1 Click on the **Insert Table** icon of the Standard toolbar (Fig. 8.1).

2 A schematic table composed of five columns and four rows appears (Fig. 8.2). To select the number of rows and columns, place the cursor in the bottom right-hand cell. Keep the mouse button pressed and drag the table diagonally until it shows the correct layout (Fig. 8.3).

Figure 8.1

Place the cursor on the Insert Table icon of the Standard toolbar.

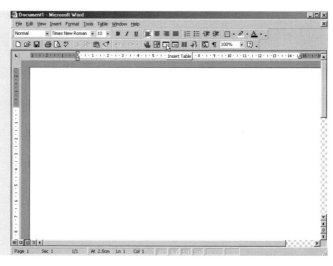

Figure 8.2

Click on the icon to insert a table and design it yourself.

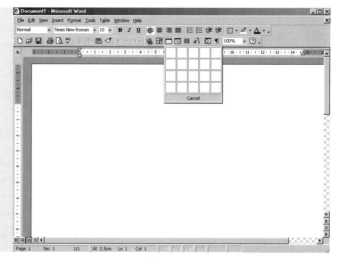

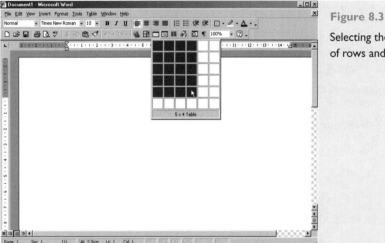

Figure 8.3

Selecting the number
of rows and columns.

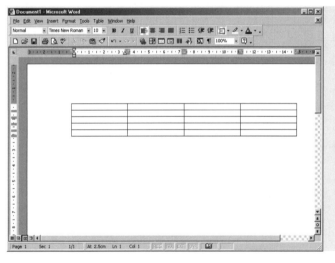

Figure 8.4

The table is inserted
into your page.

3 Let go of the mouse button and a table will appear in your
 document (Fig. 8.4).

To enter your text, put the cursor in the relevant cell and type. To
move to the next column, use the right-arrow key or the **Tab** key.

Selecting a cell

To select a cell, click on the cell selection area between the left border of the cell and the beginning of the cell text.

When a cell is selected, its background becomes black, and the text white (Fig. 8.5).

Changing the size of a cell

To change the height of a cell:

1 Select the cell.

2 Move the cursor over the top or bottom border of the cell until it becomes two arrows pointing up and down.

3 Keeping the mouse button pressed, drag this cursor up or down until the cell is the right height.

To change the width of a cell:

1 Select the cell.

2 Move the cursor over the left or right border of the cell until it becomes two arrows pointing left and right (Fig. 8.6).

3 Keeping the mouse button pressed, drag the cursor left or right until the cell is the right width.

Figure 8.5

A selected cell in your table appears in reverse.

buy	buys	bought	bought
lie	lies	lay	lain
cry	cries	cried	cried
lay	lays	laid	laid
see	sees	saw	seen

Figure 8.6

Using the cell boundary to change the cell with.

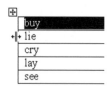

buy	buys	bought
lie	lies	lay
cry	cries	cried
lay	lays	laid
see	sees	saw

Figure 8.7

Selecting a column.

Selecting text

To select a row, double-click on the cell selection area of any cell in the row.

To select a column, place the cursor at the top of the first cell in the column, so that it becomes a black arrow pointing downwards, and click (Fig. 8.7).

Alternatively, click in the column, then select **Table**, **Select**, **Column**.

To select the whole table:

1 Click in the bottom right-hand cell.

2 Keeping the mouse button depressed, drag the cursor up and left towards the first cell in the table.

Alternatively, you can click in the table, then select **Table**, **Select**, **Table**.

Modifying the size of a table

Inserting rows

To insert a row:

1 Select the row above which you want to insert a new row. The Insert Table button in the Standard toolbar will change name and appearance and become the Insert Rows button.

2 Click on the **Insert Rows** button (Fig. 8.8).

Alternatively, you can use the Table menu to insert new rows:

1 Place the insertion point anywhere in the row above or below which you want to insert a new row.

2 Open the **Table** menu and select **Insert**.

3 Select **Rows Above** or **Rows Below**, depending on where you want the new row to go (Fig. 8.9).

Inserting columns

To insert a column:

1 Select the column to the left of which you want to insert a new column. The Insert Table button in the Standard toolbar changes into the Insert Columns button.

2 Click on the **Insert Columns** button.

Figure 8.8

Adding a row with the Insert Rows button.

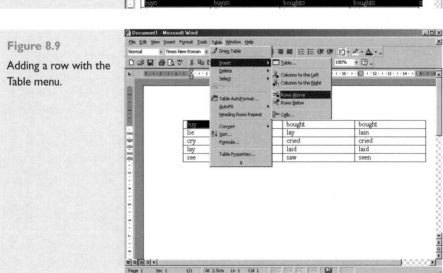

Figure 8.9

Adding a row with the Table menu.

Deleting rows

To delete one or more rows:

1 Select the row or rows that you want to delete.

2 Move your cursor into the highlighted area, and press the right-hand mouse button.

3 Select the **Delete Rows** option (Fig. 8.10). The selected row(s) will be deleted immediately.

Alternatively, you can delete rows with the Table menu:

1 Select the row or rows you want to delete.

2 Open the **Table** menu and select the **Delete** option.

3 Select **Rows** (Fig. 8.11). The selected row(s) will be deleted immediately.

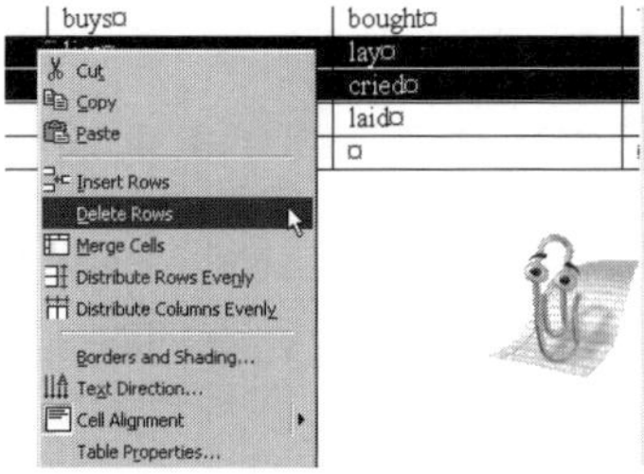

Figure 8.10

Deleting rows with the Table context menu.

Figure 8.11

You can delete rows with the Table menu.

Deleting columns

To delete one or more columns:

1 Select the column or columns you wish to delete.

2 Place your cursor inside the highlighted area, and right-click.

3 Select the **Delete Columns** option.

Alternatively, you can delete columns with the Table menu:

1 Select the column or columns you want to delete.

2 Open the **Table** menu and select the **Delete** option.

3 Select **Columns**.

Moving rows and columns

To move a row or column:

1 Select the row or column.

2 Place the cursor on the selected cells.

3 Keeping the mouse button pressed, drag the cursor to the desired new location.

Enhancing the appearance of a table

Distributing columns and rows evenly

To distribute the columns evenly:

1 Select the columns.

2 Open the **Table** menu.

3 Click on **AutoFit**.

4 Select **Distribute Columns Evenly** (Fig. 8.12).

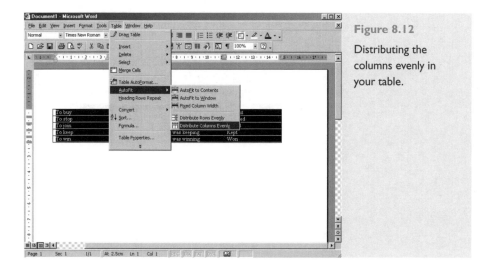

Figure 8.12

Distributing the
columns evenly in
your table.

To distribute the rows evenly:

1 Select the rows.

2 Open the **Table** menu.

3 Click on **AutoFit**.

4 Select **Distribute Rows Evenly**.

Merging cells

To insert a title row that spreads over the full width of your table,
you need to insert a row and then merge its cells. Insert the row as
shown earlier.

To merge the cells of this row into one:

1 Select all the cells to be merged.

2 Open the **Table** menu.

3 Select **Merge cells** (Fig. 8.13).

To add a title, simply type the text into the merged row, then centre
it by clicking on the **Center** icon.

Figure 8.13

Merging cells in your table.

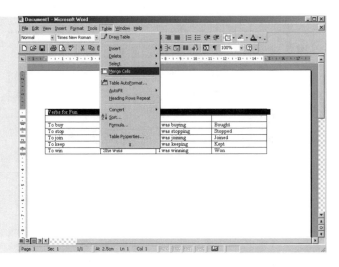

Figure 8.14

Add shading to your table.

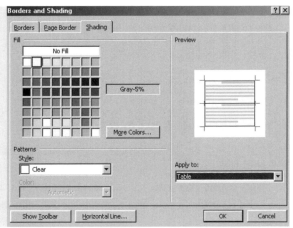

Adding shading

To add shading to the table:

1 Select the cells that you want to shade.

2 Open the **Format** menu.

3 Select **Borders and Shading**.

4 Click on the **Shading** tab (Fig. 8.14).

5 Choose your shading colour.

6 In the **Style** section, select the type of shading.

7 Click on the drop-down arrow of the **Apply to** list.

8 Select the part of the document that you wish to add the shading to.

9 Press the **OK** button.

Adding a border

You can add a border to one or more sides of a table. This can be a standard border, or it can comprise pictures. You can also embellish your table with text boxes, AutoShapes, drawings or imported ClipArt.

To add a border:

1 Click anywhere in the table.

2 Open the **Format** menu.

3 Select **Borders and Shading**.

4 Click on the **Borders** tab (Fig. 8.15).

5 In the **Setting** and **Preview** areas, select the edges that you wish to embellish with a border.

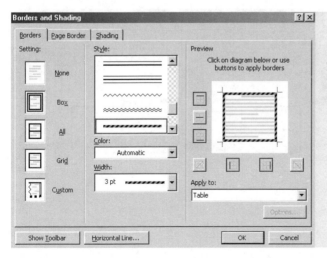

Figure 8.15

Specify a border for your table using the Borders and Shading dialogue box.

6 Customise your border by setting style, colour and width.

7 Click the drop-down button of the **Apply to** list.

8 Select the part of the table that you want to add the border to.

9 Confirm your settings by pressing **OK**.

To remove the black ¹/₂ point table border displayed by default, perform steps 1 to 4, click on **None** in the **Setting** area and **Table** in the **Apply to** list; then confirm with **OK**.

Displaying or hiding the grid

If your table is set to have no borders, cells are shown separated by fine, dotted gridlines that help you to see which cell you are working in. These gridlines will not appear on the printed page.

To hide these gridlines:

1 Open the **Table** menu.

2 Click on the **Hide Gridlines** option (Fig. 8.16).

Conversely, if you want to display the grid, click on **Show Gridlines**.

Figure 8.16

The Hide Gridlines option.

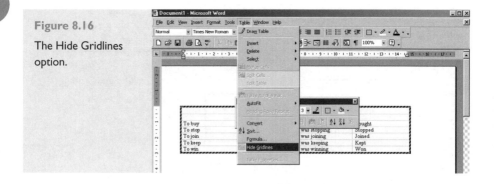

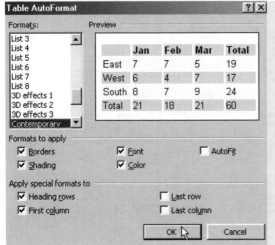

Figure 8.17

The Table AutoFormat dialogue box.

AutoFormat

The AutoFormat command applies a preset format to a table.

1 Select the table.

2 Open the **Table** menu.

3 Click on **Table AutoFormat** (Fig. 8.17).

4 Select the format you want to apply.

Converting a table to text

When a table is converted into text, the columns are replaced by tabs, commas, paragraph markers, or other characters.

1 Select the rows (or the whole table) that you wish to convert into text.

2 Open the **Table** menu.

3 Click on **Convert Table to Text**.

4 Select the separating character that you want to use.

5 Click **OK**.

Figure 8.18

Performing calculations in Word 2000.

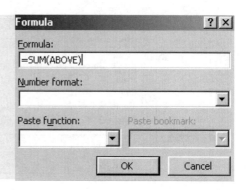

Calculating the sum of a row or column

To perform additions in your table:

1 Click in the cell where the total should appear.

2 Open the **Table** menu.

3 Select the **Formula** option (Fig. 8.18). If the cell you selected is at
   the bottom of a column of numbers, Word offers you the **= SUM
   (ABOVE) formula**. If the selected cell is at the extreme right of
   a row of numbers, Word offers you the **= SUM (LEFT)
   formula**.

4 Click **OK** to confirm.

Creating freehand tables

Being able to design a table freehand is a real advantage. In Word
2000, you can easily create columns and rows, arrange them and
modify them using the Draw Table tool:

1 In the Tables and Borders toolbar, select the **Draw Table**
   (pencil) icon.

2 Keeping the left mouse button depressed, draw the rectangle that
   will hold the table.

3 Draw the columns and rows one by one. As you begin, each horizontal or vertical line is shown as a dotted line. Release the mouse button and the column or row border will appear.

4 Use the **Eraser** icon in the Tables and Borders toolbar to remove any errors.

5 To turn off the Draw Table or Eraser option, just reclick on the **Draw Table** or **Eraser** icon.

Tables within tables

One of the more interesting innovations in Word 2000 is the possibility of creating tables within tables.

1 Select the cell to contain the subtable.

2 Click on the **Split Cells** icon in the Tables and Borders toolbar.

3 In the dialogue box that appears, specify the number of rows and columns for the new table (Fig. 8.19).

4 Click **OK**.

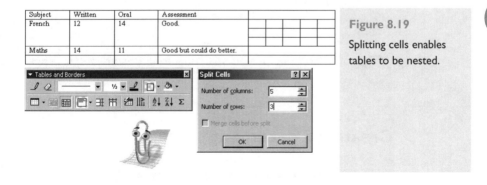

Figure 8.19

Splitting cells enables tables to be nested.

9

Outline view

- **Creating a document outline**
- **Displaying hierarchy levels in Outline view**
- **Collapsing or expanding an outline**
- **Promoting or demoting levels**
- **Moving paragraphs**
- **Selecting text in Outline view**
- **Numbering an outline**
- **Printing an outline**

 utline mode helps you structure long documents. It assigns levels to titles, and clarifies your document design and layout.

Creating a document outline

There are three ways to create a document outline:

1 Enter the headings in Outline view, then drag the + and – symbols that appear on the screen to set the appropriate heading levels.

2 Assign hierarchical levels to paragraphs in Normal view.

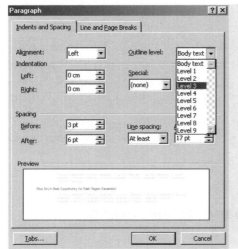

Figure 9.1

The Outline levels of the Indents and Spacing tab.

3 Create an Outline style numbered list, by using the **Format**, **Bullets and Numbering**, **Outline Numbered** function.

We will use option 2.

1 In Normal view, select the text that you want to assign an Outline level to.

2 Open the **Format** menu.

3 Click on **Paragraph**.

4 Select the **Indents and Spacing** tab (Fig. 9.1).

5 Click the **Outline level** drop-down arrow, and choose the level you want to assign to the text.

6 Click **OK**.

7 Repeat for each section of text.

Displaying hierarchy levels in Outline view

Having completed the preliminary work, go into Outline view. The structure of your document appears level by level.

The Outline view toolbar lets you display the headings up to a certain level, e.g. clicking on the **1** icon will show only level-1 headings, and clicking on the **6** icon will show all headings up to level 6.

If you click on the **All** button, the whole of your document appears with its Outline levels.

The **Show First Line Only** button displays the structure of your document, plus the first line of each paragraph.

The **Show Formatting** button (A/A) displays the formatting in your document.

Collapsing or expanding an outline

The **Collapse** icon takes the Outline down one level, e.g. if you are currently displaying level-6 headings, clicking on Collapse will display level-5 headings.

The **Expand** icon takes the Outline up one level.

Promoting or demoting levels

To promote a heading to the next level up, click on the **Promote** icon (green left arrow).

To demote a heading to the next level down, click on the **Demote** icon (green right arrow).

Moving paragraphs

The Move Up (green up arrow) and Move Down (green down arrow) icons let you move whole paragraphs up or down with one click.

In Outline view, put the cursor in the paragraph to be moved. Clicking the **Move Up** icon will reposition the paragraph immediately above the preceding paragraph. Clicking the **Move Down** icon will reposition the paragraph immediately below the following paragraph.

Selecting text in Outline view

Selecting text in Outline view is different from that in Normal view.

To select a heading, its subheadings and any associated bodies of text, click on the white cross displayed to the left of the heading.

To select a heading only, place the cursor to the left of the heading. When it changes into a white arrow, click once.

To select a paragraph, click on the white square to the left of the first line of the paragraph.

To select several headings or paragraphs, place the cursor to the left of the first line of text to be selected, then drag downwards.

Numbering an outline

To number on outlined document:

1 Open the **Format** menu.

2 Select **Bullets and Numbering**.

3 Click on the **Outline Numbered** tab.

4 Select the type of numbering you would like to apply.

5 To customise the numbering system, click on **Customize** (Fig. 9.2).

6 When you have finished, click on **OK**.

7 To apply the numbering to your document outline, in Outline view select the heading levels in the usual way – the numbering will appear automatically.

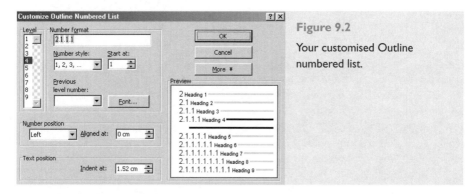

Figure 9.2

Your customised Outline numbered list.

Printing an outline

Once your document has been structured into different Outline levels, you can choose to print only the text outline or the text of specific levels.

In Outline view, display the levels you want to print. Click on **Print**.

10
Mailshots

- Creating a data file
- Printing the document
- Filtering records
- Sorting records
- Creating mailshot labels
- Printing labels from an address book

Creating a data file

A mailshot lets you create personalised documents from a database and a form letter. Your form letter is a standard Word document.

The first step is to create the form letter. Either use one of the Word templates, or write your own letter. Leave the letter document open.

The second step is to use the Mail Merge utility.

1 Open the **Tools** menu.

2 Select **Mail Merge** (Fig. 10.1).

3 Click the **Create** button.

Figure 10.1

The Mail Merge Helper dialogue box.

Figure 10.2

By clicking on Edit Data Source, you access the database to create the addresses.

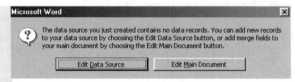

4 Choose the **Form Letters** option.

5 Choose **Active Window**.

6 Press on the **Get Data** button.

7 Click on **Create Data Source**.

Word 2000 offers a list of commonly used field names. For a mailshot addressed to clients, the LastName, Address1, City and PostalCode fields will probably be enough. To remove unwanted fields, click on the field name, then click the **Remove Field Name** button.

8 Confirm by clicking on **OK**.

9 Give your file a name in the **Filename** box.

10 A dialogue box informs you that the data source you just created contains no data records (Fig. 10.2). Choose **Edit Data Source** to access the database.

11 In the fields, enter the details for the first client.

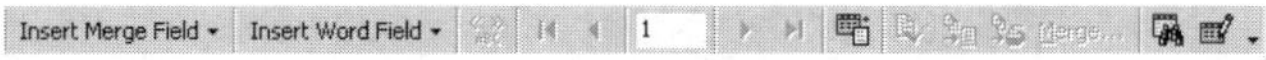

Figure 10.3
The Mail Merge toolbar.

Add this record to your database by clicking on **Add New**.

Continue adding records for the other clients.

When you have finished working, confirm your entries by clicking on **OK**.

The letter form then appears on the screen.

1 Place the insertion point in the place where the first merge field should be.

2 Expand the **Insert Merge Field** button on the Mail Merge toolbar (Fig. 10.3).

3 Select the relevant field that appears.

4 Click to confirm. The name of the field appears in your form letter.

5 Repeat this operation for the other fields.

Click on the **Merge to New Document** button to display the merge result.

Your letter and the inserted fields are instantly translated to another document.

Printing the document

If you click on the **Print** button, only the first letter will be printed.

To print the whole mailshot, go back to your merge document, and click on the **Merge to Printer** button in the Mail Merge toolbar.

Filtering records

If you do not want to merge all the information in the data file, you can set conditions for the merge. Let's say you do not want to include names that begin with A – D.

Figure 10.4

Defining your selection criteria.

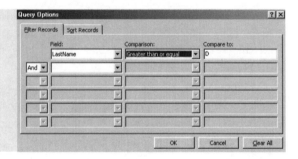

The Query options allow you to select data records from the data file. To access them:

1 Click on the **Mail Merge** button, on the right of the Mail Merge toolbar.

2 Click on the **Query Options** button.

3 Select the **Filter Records** tab (Fig. 10.4).

4 Click on the first pull-down arrow in the **Field** area and select the relevant field.

5 In the **Comparison** area, click on the **Greater than or equal** formula.

6 In the **Compare to** area, enter **D**.

To set additional selection conditions, click on **And** or **Or** to link your conditions to one another.

Sorting records

To merge records in a specific order, click on the **Sort Records** tab of the Query Options dialogue box. For example, say you want to merge the file in descending alphabetical order.

1 Click the pull-down arrow in the **Sort by** text area and select the relevant field (Fig. 10.5).

2 Tick the **Descending** button.

Figure 10.5

Sorting records.

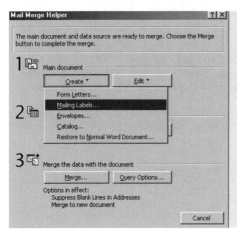

Figure 10.6

Creating mailshot labels.

Creating mailshot labels

To produce mailing labels for a mailshot, you follow the same steps as for producing the actual letter, with a couple of modifications:

1 Open the **Tools** menu.

2 Click on **Mail Merge**.

3 Open the **Create** menu.

4 Select the **Mailing Labels** option (Fig. 10.6).

5 Select **New Main Document**.

6 Click on **Get Data**.

7 Select **Create Data Source**.

8 Choose the fields you want for your labels, and click **OK**.

9 Save this file as usual.

10 Select **Set Up Main Document** (Fig. 10.7).

11 In the **Product number** area, select a label type with the same dimensions as your labels.

12 Verify the printer type.

13 Click on **New Label**

14 Enter a name in the **Label name** box.

15 Click **OK**.

The new label is listed in the **Product number** area.

16 Select the relevant fields from the **Insert Merge Field** drop-down arrow.

17 Click **OK**.

18 Select the **Merge** button.

19 Click **Merge** in the box that appears.

20 To print, click on the **Merge to Printer** icon.

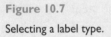
Measure the exact dimensions of your labels. The stated dimensions when purchased can vary slightly from the actual physical dimensions.

Figure 10.7

Selecting a label type.

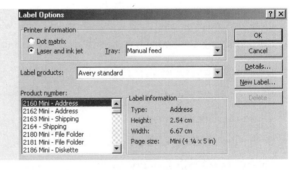

Using Word

Printing labels from an address book

To print labels from your address book:

1 Open the **Tools** menu.

2 Select **Mail Merge**.

3 Select **Create, Mailing Labels**.

4 Click on **Active Window**.

5 Select **Get Data, Use Address Book**.

6 Choose the address book you want to use and confirm by clicking on **OK**.

7 Click on the **Set Up Main Document** button.

8 Select the printer type and the type of label.

9 Insert the fields to be merged from your address book

10 Click on **Merge**.

11 Click on **Printer** in the **Merge to** pull-down box.

11
Printing

The Print dialogue box

A printer installed under Windows is automatically available in Word 2000. Printing is therefore a very simple operation.

Select the **File** menu, then click on the **Print** option. This will bring up the Print dialogue box (Fig. 11.1).

The **Name** box shows the printers that are installed on your computer. Use the drop-down arrow to select the printer you want to print on. If you have only one printer, it will already be selected.

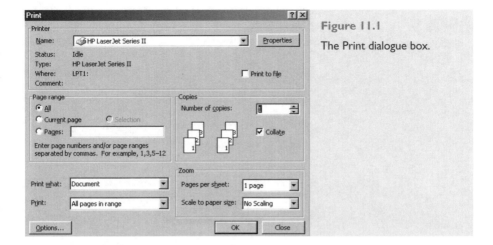

Figure 11.1

Figure 11.1

The Print dialogue box.

Selecting the text to print

To print:

1 Open the **File** menu.

2 Select **Print**.

3 In the **Page range** section, select one of the following options:

   ● **All**. The whole of your document will be printed.

   ● **Current page**. Only the page containing the insertion point will be printed.

   ● **Pages**. Specify the pages you want to be printed, e.g. to print page 3, type in **3**. To print pages 4–6, type in **4–6**.

Specifying the number of copies

To set the number of copies:

1 Open the **File** menu.

2 Select **Print**.

Figure 11.2

Printing only odd pages.

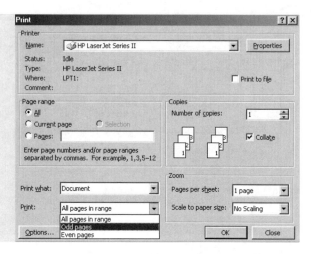

3 In the **Number of copies** field, select the number of copies you want to print. If the **Collate** option is selected, Word prints each document page by page. If the **Collate** option is not selected, Word prints all the copies of page 1, all those of page 2, etc.

Printing odd and even pages

To print only odd or even pages:

1 Open the **File** menu.

2 Select **Print**.

3 Use the pull-down arrow of the **Print** field and select one of the displayed options (Fig. 11.2).

Print options

To select the print options:

1 Open the **File** menu.

2 Select **Print**.

3 Click on the **Options** button (Fig. 11.3).

4 In the **Print** tab, select your choices by ticking the relevant boxes.

The main printing options are:

● **Draft output.** Word prints the document with minimal formatting and removes most graphics.

● **Update fields.** Updates all the fields in a document before printing it.

● **Update links.** Printing takes account of the latest changes to a linked object, e.g. a drawing (.bmp format) linked to a text file (.doc format).

● **Allow A4/Letter paper resizing.** Select this check box if you want Word to automatically adjust documents formatted for another paper size.

● **Background printing.** You can continue working while your document is printing, provided that your computer has enough RAM memory and a hard disk fast enough not to slow down your other applications. Background printing uses more system memory. To speed up printing, deactivate this option box.

● **Reverse print order.** Word 2000 prints the document starting with the last page.

Figure 11.3

The Print tab.

Printing a document's properties

You can print a document's properties, as well as things such as comments, hidden text or drawing objects.

Printing the properties without printing the document

1   Open the **File** menu.

2   Choose **Print**.

3   In the **Print what** box, choose **Document properties**.

Printing the properties and the document

1   Open the **Tools** menu.

2   Click on **Options**.

3   Select the **Print** tab.

4   In the **Include with document** section, tick the items that you want to appear in your printed document.

Cancelling printing

To cancel printing, you have three options. You can:

1   Click on **Cancel**.

2   Press **Escape** if background printing is turned off.

3   Double-click the printer button on the Status bar.

+info
If you are printing a short document and background printing is turned on, it's likely that the printer icon will not be displayed on the Status bar long enough for you to click on it!

appendix
Installing Office 2000

Office is installed using an Installation Wizard (Fig. A.I). The installation dialogue box appears as soon as the CD-ROM is inserted into the drive. After you have accepted the terms of the licence contract, the software offers two types of installation:

- **Automatic.** Office 2000 installs all the standard components, without asking you. This option is recommended for a quick and easy installation. On the other hand, there is no interaction and you have no chance of choosing an installation folder, or a choice of different components. The components can, however, be customised afterwards.

> You are strongly advised to defragment your hard disk before installing any large software application. This reduces read head movements on the hard disk and speeds up program execution. To perform this disk maintenance procedure, click on **Start**, point to **Programs**, **Accessories**, **System Tools** and select **Disk Defragmenter**. If you would like to know more about this command, consult your Windows 98 documentation.

- **Custom.** You can choose the installation folder for Office 2000 and specify the component applications you want to use. This option should be chosen if you want to keep all or part of a previous version of the program.

If you choose the Custom option, Office 2000 displays the dialogue box shown in Fig. A.2. The upper text zone contains the path leading to the folder where Office will be installed. If the default path does not

Figure A.1

Installing Office 2000.

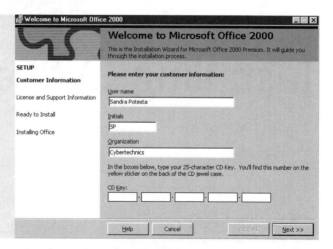

Figure A.2

If you select the custom installation, you can choose the hard disk and folder in which to install Office 2000.

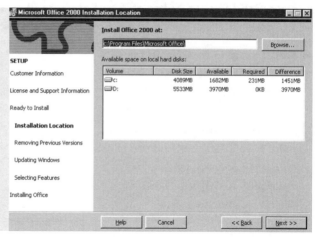

suit you, click on the **Browse** button. Windows offers you the usual tree of folders in which you can navigate to the one you want.

If the folder to hold Office 2000 does not exist yet, type its name in the text input box, being careful to separate the other folders in the path with a backslash (\). The wizard will create it automatically.

The window shows available hard disks, their size, available space, space needed for a complete Office 2000 installation, and the space that will be left over after installation. Note that the disk occupation calculations relate only to the disk named in the text input box, the

C disk in this case. If you want to install Office 2000 on another disk, you have to show it in the text input box.

The dialogue box shown in Fig. A.3 is the most important in the procedure – it is here that you choose which components to install: Word, Excel, Access, PowerPoint, as well as various tools and files.

Select all the components you want to install. If they are indispensable, install them on the hard disk. If you think you may need them occasionally, set their icon to **Install only at the occasion of first use**. Then when you need one of these components, Office will install the requested component.

If there are some elements you do not want to install, choose the **Not available** option. They will not be installed, unless you reinsert the original Office 2000 CD-ROM and choose the **Add/Remove Components** option in the Maintenance dialogue box.

Click on the **Install** button to transfer to the hard disk whatever must be transferred.

It's likely that a dialogue box entitled **Remove Shared File?** (Fig. A.4) will appear during the installation. This signals that Office 2000 is preparing to replace an existing file with one of its own. By default, the Office 2000 installer advises to keep the existing file, which is normal since it does not pose any problem. Click on **Yes** to keep it. Choose the **Yes To All** option for keeping everything, if this is offered.

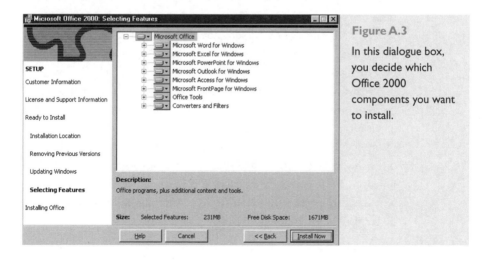

Figure A.3

In this dialogue box, you decide which Office 2000 components you want to install.

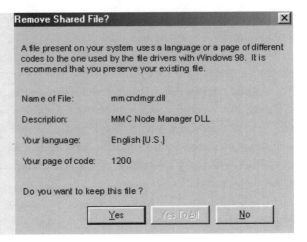

When it has finished, the Office 2000 installer signals that it must restart the computer so that Windows can register the different program elements that have been installed. Click on **Yes**.

Installation on demand

Installation on demand is a new feature of Office 2000. Until now, you had to choose the elements for installation on the hard disk. If, at the time of installation, certain files were judged to be superfluous, there was a strong risk of not thinking about them again later and even forgetting that they were ever on the CD-ROM. Other users transferred everything to the hard disk just in case, which wastes a lot of space.

With Installation on demand, the elements and files that are not installed are listed in the menus and dialogue boxes of Office 2000 applications, although they do not exist on the hard disk so they take up no valuable space. The first time you call for a function that has not been installed, the Office Assistant will display the message, 'This function is not currently installed. Do you want to install it now?'. If you want to install it, click on Yes. The Assistant will then ask you to insert the Office 2000 CD-ROM.

When a complete application has been marked with the **Install only at the occasion of first use** icon, it is also listed in the Start menu. It is only when you want to use it that Office 2000 will ask you to insert the CD-ROM for its installation.

Maintaining Office 2000

It is possible to add or remove Office 2000 components at any time. To do this, insert the original CD-ROM. If the CD does not start automatically, double-click on the file Setup.exe, in its root folder. A maintenance dialogue box (Fig. A.5) then offers several options:

● **Repair Office.** If an application does not work because it lacks a file, or because it has been damaged, this option should be selected. Missing or defective files are then replaced by their equivalents, transferred from the original CD-ROM (which must be inserted in the drive). Two options are offered in the dialogue box:

  ● reinstallation of Office 2000;

  ● repair of errors that might have occurred during installation.

Figure A.5

Restarting Office 2000 from the CD-ROM displays the dialogue box giving access to maintenance.

Generally, you will select the second option. This leaves untouched any personal files you have created in the meantime and preserves preferences set for each application.

- **Add or Remove Features.** This button gives access to the dialogue box when you select elements for installation immediately or at the time of first use. If some elements have been marked as Not available, it is possible to make them accessible again.

- **Remove Office.** This button completely uninstalls Microsoft Office 2000 from the hard disk. Personal files are kept, however.

An installation is never final. At any time, you can modify it, remove or add components, and configure Office 2000 to meet your current needs.

index